بِسْمِ اللهِ الرَّحْمَنِ الرَّحِيْمِ

عائشة

Title: My Daily Life by Ayesha (English Version)

Author: Ayesha Ghada Kanaan

Editor: Nilufer Kurtuldu

(Freelance Editor, Inspire Educate Support - IES, info@iesprograms.com)

Graphic Designers: Amanda Reynold & Monica Toscas

Publisher: Kanaan Kanaan

My Daily Life
by Ayesha

Ayesha Ghada Kanaan

Table of contents

Glossary

Asr: Mid-afternoon prayer

Dua: Verbal prayer or supplication

Fajr: Dawn prayer

Isha: Night prayer

Maghrib: Sunset prayer

Quraan: Holy Book of Muslim Faith

Zuhr: Noon prayer

In the morning

I wake up at seven o'clock
and then I pray Fajr.

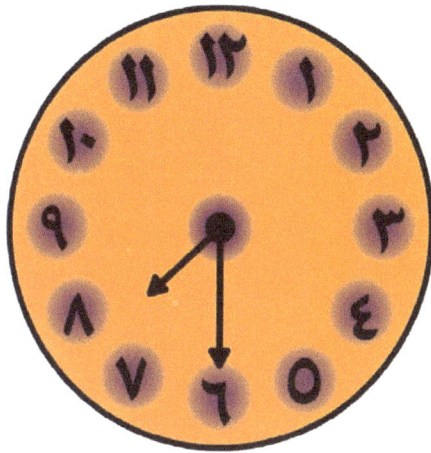

I put on my school uniform at half-past-seven.

Then, I have my breakfast at ten-to-eight.

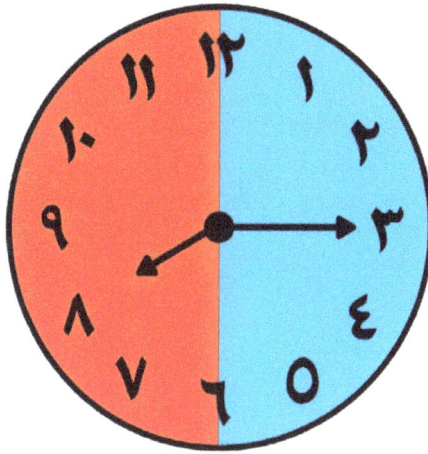

I go to school by car & I arrive at quarter-past-eight.

At five-to-nine I am in my classroom

Darul-Ulum College of Victoria

In the afternoon

In the evening

I do my homework from twenty-to-seven until seven o'clock.

Then, I pray Maghrib at eight-thirty.

At night-time

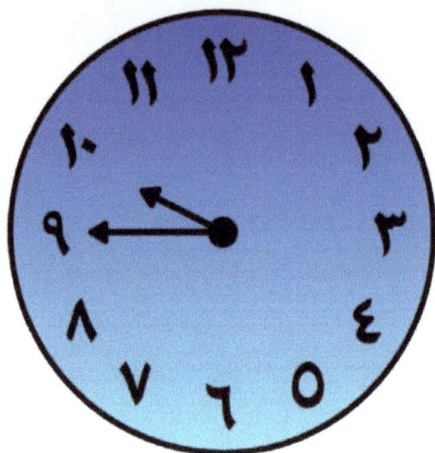

I pray Isha at quarter-to-ten.

I say my dua & go to sleep
at quarter-past-ten.

Post-reading activities

Now that you have read the book, please answer the following questions:

1. When does Ayesha get up in the morning?

....

2. How does she go to School?

....

3. Which Prayer does she do at School?

....

4. What does she do at four-twenty?

....

5. What time does she read the Quraan?

....

6. What does she do before she goes to bed?

....

7. Write something that you do in your day.

....

Completed, by the grace of Allah.

عائشة